Ousmane BA

KING OF THE ROUND BALL, FOLLOWING THE STEPS OF SADIO MANE, THE CHILD OF BAMBALI

Sadio Mane was born on April 10th 1992 in Bambali, a village located in the region of Sedhiou in Senegal. In this small rustic village located in the Natural Casamance the dominants daily activities of the villagers are fishing but especially the banana plantations which support the population as well as the cultivation of groundnuts and potatoes, etc. It is in this small locality where everything has started for the king of the soccer round ball and team of the Senegal National team for more than ten years now. Bare feet on sandy playgrounds, it's in this very particular place that Sadio has hit the ball for the first time.

Nicknamed Nanthio as a reference to the Nanthioya of the ancient Gaabu kingdom. Nanthio is actually the son of a Nanthio woman. He is among the warriors designated to ride white horses in order to wage war in expansion campaigns of the kingdom. The Nanthios has supernatural powers and a code of honor that they have respected until the late eighteenth century. The family name of the Kaabu Nanthio was generally "Sané" or "Mané". Therefore, according to his social origins, Sadio Mané is a Nanthio. A social trait will certainly appear on the playground when Sadio Mané, at an early age started falling in love with the ball. At a young age, he would only swear by the football. All his efforts and actions went into that direction. Though, he comes from an area which had never had a star football player before, a soccer player who played in the big European championships, the young Mané was certainly hopeful that one day, his dream would come true. But his family members did not agree with him. They were against his football ambitions namely his father who was a Muslim devotee, worthy pious and respectful man in their village. Hs father did not approve Mane's ambitions, that's why he tried to dissuade him, for his father Sadio was not on the straight path. His parents thought that he would study and become a teacher. For them, football was a silly game, a waste of time, but Sadio persisted in his ambitions and he has never doubted that football is the work which will allow him to support his family and relatives. He was then convinced that he would be a football player. His convictions, resilience and above all his temper will be the driving forces behind his particular success story.

Left alone, he couldn't understand why none allow him to pursue his dream and live his passion. In fact, Sadio used to live with uncle because his parents, having already many children, were short of means and couldn't make the ends meet His uncle had a team named Kansalla and Sadio was a big fan of that team. He would enjoy watching the Kansalla team play. Their playground was just about two blocks from his home. Even as a football team manager, Sadio' uncle did not like seeing his nephew play football. In fact, he did not want to dishonor the decision of Sadio's parents. He told the same thing to Sadio, which was to stay focused on his studies and let alone the football games. In spite of his challenging childhood and the fact of living in modest family the young boy had big dreams for the future.

Since his young age, he had understood that to succeed in life one should strongly believe in themselves and work really hard. Perseverant, enduring and resilient, he has always believed that anything is possible in life. Between school and the fields, Sadio used his free time to develop football skills on the streets of Bambali.

A well-mannered, respectful and a little shy but highly motivated, the young Nanthio carried out his obligations which were going to school, to the fields and to the training. It often happened to him to stop taking classes in order to go and play football. But once at home, his parents would hesitate to scold him just to let him that they did not appreciate his passion. On his way to the fields, he took all the objects such as grapefruits and stones that could be used as a balloon to play and enjoy himself. As an amusement object, his uncle bought a ball for the young Sadio, and the latter could barely separate himself from it. He was convinced that he would become a great football player one day. *"Sadio has always believed that he will become a professional football player, though I don't know on what that was based. From the get-go I didn't believe him because it was very complicated when our parents did not want to see us play football. The priority for was the field work. When he told me that he wanted to become professional football player I replied that he should follow the advice of his parents and let down this dream. But he ended up following his heart and fortunate he has made it".*

Sadio Mané was not a lazy boy, all of his actions were seriously carried out. He was a workaholic and when it was time to work in the field he was always there with his uncle. And each time he showed his uncle his ardent desire to leave the fields and get his family out of the clutches of poverty but his uncle didn't really see it as Sadio did. But Sadio did never doubted that one day he would succeed in the football world. He strongly believed in himself even if nobody was there to help him in that direction. One day while he was only seven years old, Sadio was playing football with his friends, his brother approached him and announced him the death of his father, "*I was seven years old and playing football in the streets of my villages, my brother informed me that my father had just passed away. I couldn't believe my ears; my father was just suffering from stomachs. As we didn't have a hospital in our village, he was brought to traditional healer in another village but there were some complications and finally passed away there[1].*"

Torn apart and saddened by the death of his dear father, Sadio Mané understood that he had to utmost to get his family out of hardships which they were going through. He couldn't stay there without doing something. On the contrary, he decides to work harder in the in his field passions him, the world of dreams, ambitions and motivations, namely playing football and doing everything to become a professional football player in the great clubs of the world. It was for him, the only alternative to pull his family from poverty.

---

[1] Sadio Mané, Canal + Afrique 01/31 /2020

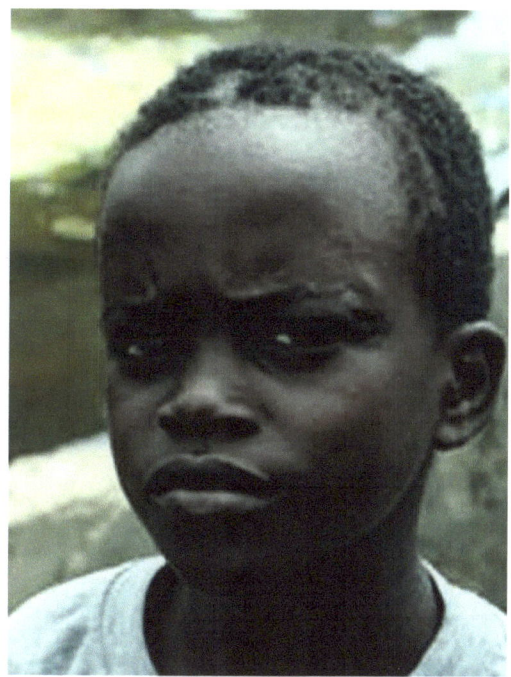

2002 WORLD CUP, THE SOURCE OF INSPIRATION

Africa's Vice champion three months earlier in Mali, the Senegal National team took part for the first time in history, to the World Cup which was organized in Japan and South Corea. On May 31, 2002, Senegal faces France, then World Cup defending champion and viewed as the favorites of the competition. Surprisingly and against all expectations, it was the Lions of the Teranga, Senegal's National team which wins the match thanks to the goal scored by the skilled and strong midfielder Pape Bouba Diop[2].

Actually, around the 30th minutes of the first half-time the ball is seized from the International French Youri Djorkaef, Elhadj Diouf then playmaker of Senegal's National picks the ball on the left side and quickly dribbles Frank LeBeouf then gave an assist to Pape Bouba Diop. The latter one does it twice before misleading Fabien Barthez despite the come back of another French defender Emanuel Petit. Towards the corner flag, the Senegalese players gather to dance around the scorer's shirt while throughout Senegal and everywhere around the world millions of fans were celebration this great

---

[2] May his soul rest in Peace, Pape Bouba Diop passed away on November 29th, 2020. He will never be forgotten by the Senegalese and African Football fans. Statutes, monuments and Public places are named after him.

exploit of Senegal's National team. Despite their fire attack composed by Thierry Henry, Sylvain Wiltord, David Trézeguet or Djibril Cissé, the French Team could not settle the score even less win the match. At the final whistle, Senegal won one goal to zero. It was the feast all around Senegal and in some parts of the world. A victory that will remain forever in the annals of Senegalese football, and it comes a turning point in the history of Senegalese football. Afterwards, the Senegalese national team keeps their performances and surprises more than one. In their second group match, Senegal managed a draw against Denmark and another draw against Uruguay. Just for the record, Uruguay knew very well that it would not be easy for them to defeat Senegal and some their players took drugs. Besides, Uruguay was caught red-handed and later suspended for two after the match because some of their players had taken drugs. After that match Senegal qualified for the round of 16. After that, Senegal faces another big team, that of Sweden. Very determined and behaving like lions in the African Savannah, the Senegalese players defeat Sweden two goals to one and end up in the quarterfinals. Something that is extremely rare for an African team. The first such thing happened was in 1990 when the Cameroon of the great Roger Milla, after defeating strong team such as Argentine and Colombia, qualified to the quarterfinals. Unfortunately for them, they were eliminated after a match which was far from being fairly refereed. The second was with Senegal during this 2002 World Cup. For the third and last time, Ghana of Assamoha Gyan which missed it against Uruguay in 2014. Coming back to this quarterfinals match of Senegal in the 2002 world cup, it was against a very strong Turk team that, in spite of all the missed occasions, came to a draw at the end of the regular full time. It was after three minutes of the overtime when one of the Turk attackers namely Ilan Mansiz managed to elude the vigilance of Senegalese defenders and ended the dream of a whole people which saw their team reach a level which have never been reached by an African team and maybe qualify for the final and win the World cup. But at that time conceding a goal during the overtime did not let any chance to settle the score. People would tell it the goal of death, meaning the first team to score during the overtime minutes win the match. If that rule of the game was in favor of Senegal against Sweden during the round of 16, it was out of their favor in against Turk. After the goal of Turk, the referee blew the final whistle and differed the Senegalese dream of playing the semifinals against the strong team of Brasilia composed of skillful players like Ronaldo, Cafu to name but a few.

Not only was this adventure of the Lions of Senegal in 2002 World Cup a success but also it also had other positive consequences for the Senegalese football specially for the youths such as Sadio Mané who wanted to become great professional football players. In fact, thanks to this competition and the never-to-be-forgotten performances of the Lions of Teranga, the young boy Sadio Mané aged 10 was really impressed and fascinated. His ambitions and dreams of becoming a professional football player became higher. He wants absolutely to follow the footsteps of these brave Senegal lions who have hit the headlines and raised the country to the highest heights in the world. Thanks to their outstanding performances, Senegal is better known in the world and many tourists dream to visit it. All this has been increased Sadio's ambition to become a professional football player and defend the flag of Senegal. His envy to become a football become stronger and he really believes in himself. If Fadiga, Bouba Diop, Tony Sylva, Henri Camara to name but a few succeeded such an exploit and became the flag-bearers of a whole nation or even an entire continent, "why not me" would say the young Sadio. Really impressed by this strong and beautiful team of his country, Sadio Mané is absolutely convinced that his destiny is in the football world. His name Sadio Mané, the child of Bambali, Casamance and Africa must be known not only in Senegal but also in Africa and throughout the entire world. With such a determination and motivation, nothing is out of reach and nothing can stop him.

CHILDHOOD AND YOUTH OF SADIO MANE

From now on, Sadio Mane and the young boys in village take football. They play in the streets of their village with other young boys. To have much

Image1 : The Teranga Lions celebrating a goal against France in the opening game of the 2002 football World Cup in South Correa.

Image2: Senegal's win against Sweden in the eighth finals in the 2002 World Cup.

Image 3: Senegal against Denmark. 2002 World Cup. 2nd match of the stage group.

Image 4: Quarter final match, Senegal against Turkish during the 2002 World Cup. The fabulous journey of Lions stops for the Lions.

more to play, they decide to hold a little tournament during the holidays inside their village, that tournament is also known as "navetanes" in Senegal, meaning the big school holidays and during the rainy seasons between July and October. Fast, highly technical, endowed with a remarkable power of strike and a keen sense of game management of his team, Sadio did not delay to make a show of himself. He began becoming the favorite of football fans who came in mass to watch these tournaments. He becomes more and more determined to be the best player of the tournament and win each match. Fast, technical and challenging the young Nanthio quickly becomes the favorite player of the public of Bambali. After watching the 2002 world cup and the outstanding performance of Senegal's national team, Sadio is blown out by the star of the Senegalese team, El-hadji Diouf, the magician of the round ball, tactician, tricky dribble, difficult to match, efficient goal-scorer and assists provider. Elhadj Diouf who conquered the hearts of all Senegalese is also appreciated by the round ball's fans in some parts of Africa and in the world. In 2002, Diouf was at the peak of his career. The Lions' star naturally became the role model of Sadio Mané. Apart from the Senegalese attacker Elhadji Diouf, Sadio Mané really admires the Brazilian magician Ronaldinho. "*I would rather say that it is this world cup (2002) that has motivated much more, I remember when we were at primary school with my friends at the end of the school year, it was on May 31st I think, we had let everything and went to watch the match opposing Senegal to France, it was great*".

THE RUNNING AWAY

Having dreams is something but making them come true is something else. Being conscious that staying in his native Bambali wouldn't help him

Image 5: Bambali local young team: This is where everything started for Sadio Mane.

Image 6: Elhadj Diouf, Sadio's idol

Image 7: Ronaldinho a great Brazilian start, a player who has inspired Sadio Mane

realize his dream, the young Sadio decided to go to the biggest city of Senegal, the capital city Dakar in order to try his luck in in the football profession. A man from his village told him that he had a friend in Dakar who manages a football team and that Sadio could go and there. As his family hadn't so far approved his passion, Sadio Mané decided to go without letting them know. He carefully and discreetly prepared his travel bag to hide it in the herbs in order not to be surprised. As he didn't have money to pay his transport, he borrowed it from one of his friends. Early in the morning, he left for Dakar without informing none except his best friend. Once in Dakar, he was lucky to be accepted in the trainings and show his skills. He did some very encouraging training sessions. One week later, all his family was look for and asking after him. His best friend who couldn't no longer keep the secret was finally obliged to reveal it, he told them that Sadio had already gone to Dakar in order to try his luck as a football player. Sadio's family didn't delay to ask for a number phone where you could join him. They called him and beg him to return to the village, but the Bambali child didn't want to go back home. However, he felt a little guilt and was somehow shameful of having gone without the green light of his parents who were really worried about. He decided finally to lend an ear to his family accept to return to Bambali.

Seeing that their beloved little one was close to anything to achieve his goal including putting his life at risk by traveling without resources, Sadio's family was then obliged to listen to the young boy and support him so that he succeed in the football world as it is the only thing that he loves and spends his time and energy on. Sadio who had just 15 years got then the blessings of his dear mother along with those of his other relatives in Bambali.

TOWARDS THE PROFESSIONAL WORLD

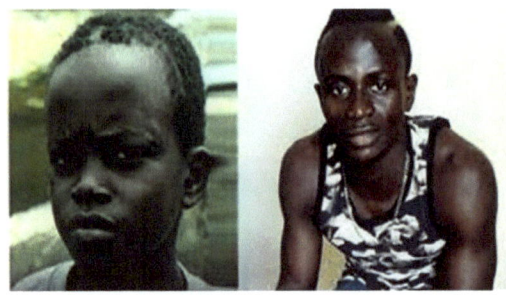

Image 8: Sadio Mane, a bold teenager who decides to take charge of his own future

Image 9: Generation foot, a Football training center where Sadio did his first tests before being recruited

Sadio Mané was playing a football match during a departmental tournament when he was noticed by a players' scout who came to the city of Mbour located on the small Senegalese coast about 100 miles from Dakar. As soon as the latter saw Sadio Mané play, he was impressed and convinced by the skills of the young man. From that day, he knew that a brighter future in the football profession ahead of Sadio Mané. And the players' scout did not hesitate to invite Sadio to play in his club in Mbour. This is what Sadio's uncle said about it: *"I remember on his departure to Generation Foot we were in a departmental tournament, that day Sadio played well and even did an assist which allowed our team to win the match. After the match a guy from Mbour suggested that he wanted Sadio Mané to come with him. After he had the approval of his family, the Nanthio went with the guy. He helped the team to join the league and scored two goals in a junior cup game. It was that day that he was spotted by the recruiters from Generation Foot and these latter invited him to participate in the tests".* By persuasion, the child of Bambali ended up convincing his family to let him go and meet the trainers. He took care of all the administrative procedures and prepared all that was necessary for his trip. It was with the electrified spirit of the dreams to success that the young man landed in Mbour, there was the biggest youth training football center of the country. He did wonders in this Mbour' s Team, and during a Cup match his performances did not fail to pleasantly surprise a recruiter from Generation Foot who invited him to participate to their tests. With his precarious equipment, a short and worn shoes, one of the recruiter did not miss to taunt him *"you want to become a football player like this, you don't even have the means, look how your shoes are, well I replied, that was the only things I had."* Despite the jeers and mockeries, he was experiencing, that did not prevent his talent to draw the attention of all. Sadio did extraordinary things during these crucial games for his future as professional football player. With more than three hundred young boys waiting in line most of whom had more suitable means and equipment. He had a short looked nothing like that of a football player and his shoes were all torn on the sides, even though he had repaired them as he could with a thread, those who were supervising the tests looked him down, they despised him. Fortunately for him, he was talented and ended up being selected. Abdou Diatta, a recruiter of the football center Generation Foot said something on this matter: *"when I saw his touch, I thought, this is a good player. After two days of tests I said, we are going to hire this without any delay".* That's the beginning of an adventure. During his first match, he scored four goals and all the recruiters were blown out by his talent. He integrated Generation Foot, the best training center at that time. Sadio Mané was the most motivated and regular. He was always the first to arrive at the playground, he always came on time and began working out before the others joined him. He had already understood that there is no magic secret, with hard work and determination he will end up reaching the highest peak. Disciplined, motivated, determined and self-demanding, his integration and adaptation in his team happened quickly. It's the beginning of a long way for the child of Bambali. Sadio was happy and flourishing in this center. With his qualities of percussion and speed he ended up convincing everybody in the club of Dakar. According to Dahaba Diatta, his then coach *"he is full of qualities, when you sees him playing you will immediately know that he is a good football player, in spite of the playground conditions with the rains which made hard to play on, he always managed to get away with it, with his ways of touching the ball and his dribbles, he knew really how to keep the ball. He made excellent sequences and linking, he had a remarkable talent"*. From Mbour to Generation Foot, Sadio Mané experienced a meteoric rise. He was an example to follow for the players on and out of the playground. He is described by his coaches as someone with a great asset on whom a team can count in order to go forward. In term of attack, he did exceptional things and allowed his team to move up to the second division of the Senegalese league and his performances would have him selected for the Generation Foot program, which will be his gateway to Europe. That's when he caught the eye of a youths' coach named Olivier Perrin who came from Metz. And Olivier organized his move to Metz.

MANE IN THE WORLD OF PROFESSIONAL FOOTBALL PLAYERS. His beginnings with FC Metz in France

In the middle of the winter on January 4, 2011, the young Nanthio set foot on France. He came straight from Generation Foot where he had been spotted by Olivier Perrin, then Director of Metz training center and current operating manager of Generation Foot. Olivier says: *"I would go several times to Dakar per year for the detection. It didn't take me a minute to notice that he was totally different. In his ball-picking, his capacity to eliminate many players. Individually, no comparison"*. Sadio Mané didn't take care to prevent his parents that he would go to France. Some days later after he had arrived to France, he called his mother to tell her that he was in France but she was dumbfounded and couldn't believe his ears. Every day, she called her son to see if he had told her the truth. To convince his mother that he was actually in France, he told her to watch the TV to see him play, she finally understood that the dream of the young boy has come true. Well arrived and welcomed by his elders from Generation Foot such Diawara Sakho and others, his integration in the group happened easily. Once he arrived to Europe Sadio was flabbergasted or shocked. It is less than five degrees but not enough to calm down. Unfortunately, things started badly and the young man was suffering from a recalcitrant pubalgia which he hid from his coaches by the fear of being sent back to his country of origin. The way was still long to make it but the Nanthio was determined and the injuries didn't frighten him.

He started with the U19. And for two he didn't achieve something great. He was operated and then started his adventure with garnets after six months. He began showing exceptional things that the other players couldn't do. Mathieu Duhamel was privileged witness of the rising of the Senegalese to the group of professionals: *"I would often go and see him with the reserve. And he had caught my eye. But when he started in League 2, his talent exploded in everybody's eyes"*. Within some months the talent, speed, and the dribble technics of the Native of Sedhiou impressed everyone watching him play. He was selected to the professional team and came into play for the first time on January 14th 2012 during a defeat against Bastia. FC Metz slid into a negative spiral but Sadio proved to be a great football player. In April 2002, he signed his first professional contract for four years and scored his first goal some days later. A goal and an assist in nineteen matches, his statistics was not surprising but his game plan in Metz was original. Despite his very convincing individual performances, this doesn't prevent the garnets from finishing the season in the eighteen place of the classification and undergoing a historical downhill in the third division. At the end of his first campaign, his performances earned him to play with the Senegalese National team in May 2012.

The promising promises of the young Senegalese captivated many recruiters. Many foreign clubs wanted to draw him into their nets including Reb Bull Salzburg. FC Metz was financially weakened by the relegation to

National and agreed to let their rough diamond go. It was the most important transfer since those of Robert Pires and Miralem Pjanic. This transfer enabled FC Metz to secure the balance of its accounts, maintain a quality workforce and start afresh on sound basis. But Bernard Serin, FC Metz president, is keen on his nugget: *"we really want to keep Mané, that's why I set a very high transfer allowance thinking that no club could match that amount, never achieved for a National player and even extremely for a League 2 player. It was not an easy decision to make, believe me, I couldn't decently refuse this offer. In the view of the loss of TV rights and subsidies, selling our best players and especially the best Sadio Mané was the only solution so that I did not put even more hand in the pocket"*, the president of the club said on August 31, 2012.

In addition to the performances with FC Metz, the child of Bambali had taken part to the Olympic Games in 2012 with the Hope team of Senegal. The young Sadio then aged 20, had come out of the anonymity. Indeed a few weeks on the occasions of the Olympic Games, in London, where a certain Gerald Houiller was blown out by the speed and technical qualities of this typical player viewed as a gift from God. The head of Salzburg football department had seen the twenty-year old play shine at the London Olympics with the Senegalese team. One evening in August 2012, a man in a dark jacket and thin glasses on his nose began to turn around the Saint Symphorien Stadium. He settled quickly on a plastic seat. There is a second round of the league cup between FC Metz and Tours, a match won by the Locals. This man in a dark jacket was not none other than Ralf Rangnick, the sports director of Reb Bull Salzburg. He was sent to check Houiller's favorite. Rangnick approved the profile of the young Senegalese. After the match, he went to meet the president of Metz club and the later insisted that he would not sell his nugget less than four million euro. It was a huge amount for a player who was evolving in French third division the aftermath of appointment with the boss of the club Ralf Rangnick succeeded though to convince his boss, Dentier Mateschitz to provide a financial effort. They reached an agreement and Sadio's adventure with Metz ended.

Image 10: Sadio Mane with Metz club in France

Image 11: Sadio Mane at the Olympic Games with the Team Hope of Senegal

Image 12: Sadio Mane's transfer deal from Metz to Salzburg. The deal is estimated about 20 million Euros, a record for Metz.

A POLISHED DIAMOND AT SALZBURG IN AUSTRIA

His ever-growing reputation, the winger returned to Metz after the Olympics with a handful European clubs in pursuit of his signature. Sadio chose Reb Bull Salzburg the last day of the 2012 Mercato saying this: *"Regarding my young age, I thought that it will the ideal club for me to work harder, learn and improve myself"*. On August 2012, while he was to Quevilly for a championship football match, Sadio Mané got down of the Metz bus and got on a plane for Salzburg. The young Senegalese did not even where Austria was located in a map. He had to do some research on Google to know a little more about the Austrian club, Salzburg confided Moustapha Mesloub, one of the responsible for players integration, the task of helping Sadio Mané settle in Austria. He settled in a humble apartment in town and quickly learned German. Mesloub asserts in this regard: *"I had to look permanently after him. He spent lot of time with me and my family, and became almost an adaptive child"*. It is with the Austria's club that he improved his imperfections. He really improved himself and got better in terms playing football. Yet, the Native of Bambali had a dream, which was "to write the history of Metz", too early and tickled by fate, he did not have the required time. It was in the city of Mozart, one of the greatest composers of the history of European music, that he developed his share. Accompanied by a personal assistant seconded by the club in order to foster and facilitate his integration and adaptation, the twirling became gradually another player. On the playground, he grew up consequently. Andrea Ulmer confirmed it: *"he came at a time when we were developing our style of playing, by imposing an intense pressing, and he marvelously fitted in with his dynamism, physical qualities and his technical subtlety"*. He knew that he would progress a lot at Salzburg, a thing that the club leaders had promised him. The former dynamite of Metz only needed a handful of football matches to put his new audience in his pocket, and he quickly found talented and skillful supports such as Kevin Kampl, Valon Berisha and Jonathan Soriano. *"Thanks to Sadio, we managed to change approach and develop the football that we wanted to into practice at Salzburg. From the first training sessions, we saw that we he had assets of a great football player. He had to be familiar with some tactical notions, but it didn't enough time to upgrade. I have rarely seen a hardworking and altruist player, and who put all his energy to the service of his team. It's the dream of any coach"* Schmidt said, Salzburg coach. It was there that he learned the real football and his coach really trusted him. Sadio started quickly to interact with the high level. He had an impressing way to eliminate his adversaries. His club had provided him the necessary tools, weight lifting, a carpet, ... The Nanthio was obsessed with the idea of getting better and wanted to rid of the last range of fat he left on his body, the goal was simple: the child of Bambali wanted to develop his muscles and be strong so that he can resist the many blows he receives each weekend and to gain in explosiveness. If in Metz, there were many African players in the team, and the city, it was not really the same story at Salzburg. In terms of food for example, it was a real problem because there was no African restaurant in the city. Therefore, he contented himself with pasta, for it much closer to the Senegalese food.

On the pitch the young Senegalese was in good shape, he made a thunderous entry in the Austria's Bundesliga. For his first season in the championship, he scored sixteen goals and eight assists in twenty-eight matches. He also scored a double and two triples during that season. He scored three goals in just three appearances in the Austria Cup. Overall, he had scored nineteen goals in twenty-nine matches during his very first season sous les couleurs du Reb Bull.

His second season was much more prolific in terms of goals During his 2013-2014 fiscal year, the Nanthio made a show of himself a little more with the club. He made his preliminary UEFA champions league debut, and after took part to the Europa League. In the Austria's Bundesliga during that season, the former nugget of Generation Foot had succeeded in to score thirteen goals and twelve assists in thirty-three matches. In the Austria Cup, he scored five goals in five appearances. He equally participated to the Europa League by scoring four goals and delivering two assists in nine matches. He scored the first triple of his senior career during a victory three goals to one against Kaldor at the third of the Austria's Cup on October 27th 2012. He had scored 31 goals in 63 appearances. He won the Nation Championship in 2013-2014. On record, he played fifty matches, scored twenty-three goals and gave fifteen assists.

He also experienced racism through two significant events. The first one was: the teardrops of a young boy whom Sadio had given a smile, the boy had never seen a black man so far. At Salzburg, ninety-nine of the population was composed of Whites. This incident deeply touched the young Senegalese. The second time, he went through racists abuses from an adversary during a match against SK Sturn Graz. All that contributed to shape and strengthen the character of the Nanthio, who had then become an international player. Sadio Mané proved again his huge skills in Austria where he would definitely and sportily explode during his second season namely through a friendly match against Bayern of Guardiola in January 2014, where Mané had, several times, put down Javi Martinez.

Things would turn out bad soon after, the Senegalese having become a bigger target. Knowing that he was being courted by many big clubs, the young man began to stop training with the club to force his transfer. This reference also wakened the outside world. Clubs such as Bayern started interesting him, though Bayern did not finally make a concrete deal, but also Liverpool and Borussia Dortmund. One day, Jurgen Klopp, then coach of Borussia Dortmund, moved to Salzburg to discuss with the young Mané and check out his character. He finally went back to Germany without Sadio Mané and admitted later having made one of the biggest mistakes of his life which is the fact of not recruiting the "Nugget". He started the 2014-2015 season with the

Austrian club. He already had eight appearances for three goals and five assists before his flight to Southampton in England. After the early elimination of Salzburg in the Champions League in Malmo in Sweden that season, Sadio showed his intention to leave, those who were interested in him were not lacking. The adventure of the child of Bambali continues and he finally went with Ronald Koeman, then Southampton coach.

Image 10: Sadio Mane with Metz club in France

Image 11: Sadio Mane at the Olympic Games with the Team Hope of Senegal

Image 12: Sadio Mane's transfer deal from Metz to Salzburg. The deal is estimated about 20 million Euros, a record for Metz.

A SHOOTING STAR IN ENGLAND

In September 2014, the English club Southampton brought the talented Sadio Mané in their squad for an amount of about 15 million euros corresponding to 12 million sterling. He signa a four-years-contract. Like many players, the dream to interact with the best football players pushed Mané to join Southampton. Talent unveiled in Senegal and confirmed at Metz then at Reb Bull Salzburg, it was at the Saints that he made himself known to the general public, for there, he was evolving in the best championship of the world.

During his first match with his new club, he got a penalty which contributed to Southampton's victory two goals to one against Arsenal in a League Cup match. He immediately made a difference by delivering an assist during his beginnings in the Premier League against Queens Park Rangers and then scoring his very first goal the following month. After scoring in three consecutive matches against Chelsea and Christal Place, he added up two goals at the end of the match against Christal Place and Queens Park Rangers.

He stayed about four months without find his goal scoring touch in the Premier League, the number ten of Southampton scored two goals during a win against Liverpool of Jurgen Klopp in March 2016, then scored five goals in his five following games, including two in four-goal win against Pep Guardiola's Manchester City. The best striker of Southampton scored fifteen goals in all games during that season.

SADIO MANE IN THE PREMIER LEAGUE HISTORY:

It is without any shadow of doubt that this arrival and the outstanding performances of Sadio Mané which mostly attracted the English fans during his time at Southampton. The child of Bambali went down the English Championship one Saturday afternoon. No sooner had he arrived, than he broke the records of the fastest triple of Premier League history in less than three minutes. He outperformed Anfield's former idol, Robbie Fowler, who had scored the same goals but in four minutes and thirty seconds in 1994. It was the thirty-seventh day of the Premier League; Chelsea had already won the title. The match of day Southampton and Aston Villa is therefore anecdotic for the title but important for the final classification, while he had just joined The Saints, the Senegalese secured his name in the annals of the club and the premier league history. Against Aston Villa, on May 16, 2015, the Southampton score the fastest triple of the Premier League. In two minutes and fifty-six seven seconds, he crucified Aston Vila. He opened the score in the thirteenth minutes by striking back a first shot repelled by the goalie. In the following minute, he picked off a pass and deceived the goalie before completing his work in the sixteenth minute with a powerful shot before delivering an assist in their last goal. A six-to-one-win. Who knows, without the celebrating, he might have been able to beat James Hayter's all-time record of two minutes and twenty seconds, while making it clear that James Hayter did not do it in Premier League but in the third division. No player has never been so fast in scoring goal in a such a short time. It is undoubtedly one of the favorite games in his career, a game which allowed him to show himself to a general public. For Sadio, this exploit is « a trigger », making it clear that he no longer had the right to error as he had gone to the next level and that everything was possible for then one.

During his first season he played thirty games in the Premier League and scored eleven goals. The following season, the child of Bambali pursued his way with the English elite. He scored again eleven goals and made seven assists during his thirty-seven appearances in Premier League. He equally played a game in the England Cup, two games and three goals in the English League Cup and scored a goal in three games during the UEFA championship's qualifications. Altogether, in his forty-three games in with the Saints in all competitions during his last season with them, he scored fifteen goals and made eight assists.

However, he was not spared by the anger of his coach Ronald Koeman. Actually, he was put on the sidelines during a one to zero defeat against Norwich in January 2016, after having missed the team meeting. Some members of the team staff say the reason was a little more innocent. Finally, the coach learned that he number ten was a little lost in the hotel trying to find the room where the meeting was being held, which indeed made him come late. But Ronald Koeman didn't appreciate and told him to get out of the meeting room. Anyway, Sadio's stock was increasingly and Klopp didn't forget him.

Image 14: Far from giving a crazy suspense to the football fans in the end of the season, yet, the Premier League delighted many of them. Thanks to Sadio Mane, the English League took some colours during a game opposing Southampton to Aston Villa on May 16 2015. A flashback on the success of the Saints' forward. That what could be seen on headlines of some European sportive newspapers, namely the Ducodusport newspaper.

MANE AT LIVERPOOL

Since the skillful and the talented Louis Suarez had left and with the injuries of Daniel Sturridge, Liverpool attackers had not scored the goals which indeed were expected from them. This urged Jurgen Klopp to go in the pursuit of more offensive options in the 2016 summer. On June 27 2006, the young Senegal was shown on picture, proving that he had just done his medical visit with Liverpool. On June 28 after he joined Liverpool on a deal of 30 million Sterling, Sadio Mané said: *"that it was the right moment, the right coach and the right club for him"*. Sadio's transfer is the third most expensive one in the history of the club. He becomes the third Senegalese football player to join the club after Elhadj Diouf and Salif Sadio. He was the most expensive African football player at that time and he wore the number 19. The young man did not find any challenge in imposing himself among the Firmino and Coutinho's powerful duo, together they constituted a terrible trio of death that could challenge the strongest defense in the European championship. Sadio Mané began with the Reds during their game against Barcelona, and he scored his first goal with a wonderful completion allowing the Reds to win four goals to zero. He made a sensational start by scoring a fabulous goal during his first days in the championship, a four to three win against Arsenal. He picked the ball on the left wing, eliminated two Arsenal players before sending the ball over the left corner of the nets. He missed the following match against Burnley because of an injury on the shoulder. Even though he had just come to the club, the young Senegalese quickly turned out to be a crucial player for the team. And the fans got worried when Sadio got injured during an international break Fortunately there was any danger and started during the four to one win again Leicester. On December 2016, he scored the goal of the victory at the 94th minute in a game against Merseyside. Two months later he was nominated the man of the match against Tottenham. Three weeks later, he made high level performances, scoring a goal and making an assist in a win against Arsenal. On April 2017, he scored his thirteen goal during a win against Everton. The unforgettable moments of his season came when he scored the goal of the victory in the overtime minutes in the derby at Goodison Park and two goals in two minutes against the Spurs of Tottenham at Anfield.

Thanks to his excellent performances and his crucial contribution to the Liverpool campaign, Sadio was nominated in Premier League team of the year (PFA), but was not selected for the choice of the best player of the year. As a consolation prize, Sadio was designated Liverpool player of the year by the players and the fans.

With the coming of the international Egyptian Mohamed Salah in the 2017 summer, Sadio went to the left wing, his favorite position. This paring with Roberto Firmino had been prolific in the post-season and was the favorite ahead trio of the Reds. On August 12, Sadio Mané scored the first goal of the Liverpool for the season, equalizing goal for the Reds, the match against Watford ended in a 3-3 draw. A week later, he scored the win goal during a tough game against Crystal Place. At Anfield, on August 27 the 25-year-old Senegalese became Liverpool's third player, following Robbie Fowler and Daniel Sturridge, to score during each of the three first games of the season championship, after scoring in the second Liverpool game during a four-to-zero win against Arsenal.

By his precise assists and his deep penetrations which systematically turn into a goal, Sadio Mane very quickly became indispensable within the team. After he had been missing for a month due to an injury, he came back stronger and more determined to help his team reach their objectives set. After he had stayed about a month without being on target, he scored his first goal by scoring a wonderful headed goal during a draw game against FC Seville. With the strong desire to score, he opened the score in the following match and released a crucial assist to his teammate Mohamed Salah who put the ball in the nets. As a fish in water, Mané was at the peak of his form. On December 6th, he scored a double in UEFA champion League through a 7 to 0 crushing win against Spartak Moscow. The first goal was his own admission and he said it was one the best goal of he had scored so far. Some weeks later by way of responding to the critics which were falling on his head due to his counter-performances through his two games, he scored the first goal of the win against Burnley. He continued his way by scoring Liverpool's third goal with a strong shot during a 4-3 win against the big Manchester City of the technician Pep Guardiola.

Since his arrival to Liverpool, the Reds had never regretted their choice since Mané would bring them at the peak of the victory. With his immense energy and prodigious dribbles, he was the darling of the English football fans. On February 2018, the Nanthio scored his first triple under the colors of Liverpool during a 5-0 win against Porto in UEFA Champions League. The first goal was a strong shot which escaped the goalie, while the second was an easy completion after the shot of Roberto Firmino which had rebounded. The third, however, a powerful 25 meter-strike at the end of the game which completed the victory. Mané kept the momentum during his following appearance, scoring the fourth goal against West Ham, equalizing his goals total of the previous season. He added up another one the week which followed scoring also the goal victory against Newcastle with a beautiful completion.

As usual, he scored a crucial equalizing goal during an outside win against Crystal Palace transforming a good assist from James Milner. Mane got lucky not to be expelled by a red card after having plunged and taken the ball. Four days later, as he knows how to do it, Sadio Mané scored a goal during a nice win against Man City at home in quarter-finals of UEFA Champions League. And he did the same thing in a win against Bournemouth. A superb goal, a strong close shot. Some weeks later, Sadio Mané scored Liverpool's third goal during a crazy game upon the UEFA Champions League semi-finals against Roma. He did it again at the return match in order to join the final big-eared Cup, the German coach; Jurgen Klopp long-awaited achievement.

It's done! The Bambali Child is at the UEFA champions League finale, Sadio had just realized one of dearest long-life dreams, a final game against Zinedine Zidane's Real Madrid at Kiev Olympic stadium in Ukraine. The Meringues won the game, after Sergio Ramos sent out Mohamed Salah, Liverpool outstanding finisher at that time and two balls of the Reds' goalie plus Gareth Bale's fantastic acrobatic shot. Sadio scored the single goal of his team and reached the pole in the second half. Sadio Mané finished his season with 20 goals in 44 appearances.

Image 15: 2018 Champions League Final at Kiev, Liverpool against Real Madrid, game won by Real Madrid.

2018-2019, SADIO MANE'S GLORIOUS SEASON:

Before the starting of the new campaign, the number 10 shirt was handed to Sadio Mané after Philip Coutinho had left to Barcelona. It was the beginning of the Premier League, and he score two goals against West Ham and the game ended up with a 4-0 win in favor of Liverpool. It was the third consecutive season that he had scored during the first day of the Premier League. A week later, they won against Crystal Palace scoring a goal in the overtime minutes. On September 1st, Sadio Mané scored his fourth goal in the season through many games, opening the score during a win against Leicester.

After a dazzling start to the season, Mané played eight games without being on target, before he finally made it during a 4-0 win against the Star of Belgrade. Three days later, he scored a double with two nice completions during a win against Cardiff. Some times after he continued in a fruitless sequence, playing another eight games without being on target. He broke the curse again on December 18, 2018 when Mané opened the score in 3-1 win against Manchester United with a great completion of an assist from Firmino. Two weeks later, the Nanthio took over Liverpool third goal during a 5-1 win against Arsenal, devastating the team from the inside of the surface after a perfect assist of the Egyptian Mohamed Salah.

A real war machine on the pitch just as efficient in attack, defense and terribly strong when he is position on the left wing. He caused sparks and continued to inflame the English championship. On January 12, Sadio made his 100th show for the English club during a wonderful win at Brighton. A week later, he scored his second goal of the season, put calmly the ball deep in the nets upon a victory against Crystal Place. During the following match he opened the score against Leicester and the game ended up in marks equality. The number 10 kept the momentum by scoring two goals during the two following games. It was the first time he had scored in a four-match serial in the English football. On January 27, he signed a double in the first twenty minutes through a 5-0 win against Watford, first a headed goal after a beautiful assist from Trent Alexander Arnold then he scored an audacious back heel. It was his fourteen goal in Premier League, a total that he had never reached in England.

On March 19, 2019, the Nanthio had his fiftieth goal for Liverpool, scoring crucial goals during a 4-2 against Burnley. Three days later, the winger scored his third double goal in four games, opening the goal against Bayern before completing a 3-1 win which allowed the Reds to join the quarters-final of UEFA champions league. He pursued his dazzling rise to fame and his urge to score goals became more and more ardent. He scored the first the goal against Fulham, signing thus his twentieth goal of the season; On April 28th, Sadio Mané signed allowing him to be among the golden boot nominees and maintain Liverpool in the pursuit of the title. A week later, he achieved exceptional performances when Liverpool overcame a heavy first leg defeat against Barcelona, winning the Catalan club 4 to 0 at Anfield in order to reach the UEFA championship league final for the second consecutive time. A never to be forgotten game in the history of football. The following game he scored a double against Wolves. Though his team lost the championship, Mané won his first golden boot, prize of the best striker with 22 goals sharing the prize with his teammate the Pharaoh Mohamed Salah and the International Gabonese Pierre Emerick Aubameyang from Arsenal.

On July 2019, Sadio started a second UEFA champions League final. Less than a minute later, he carried out a shot which fell on Tottenham defense Moussa Sissoko's arm, then giving Liverpool a penalty and the ball was transformed into a goal by Mo Salah. Jurgen Klopp's men ended up defeating the Tottenham Spurs on a score of 2 goals to 0. Mané then won his first trophy with the Reds. He finished the season with twenty-six goals in fifty appearances, his highest total in career and became Liverpool second best player.

After having missed the whole pre-season due to international service, Sadio Mané made his first appearance in the 2019-2020 season as a substitute during a win again Norwich. Five day later, he started as an incumbent player against Chelsea in the UEFA super Cup League. The Reds won the game after a penalty shootout, after Sadio score the two goals on a draw against Chelsea. On August 17, 2019, Sadio made his first start in Premier League season, against his club, Southampton. Despite a challenging first half time of Liverpool, Sadio Mané boosted them at the top position with a powerful shot in the farthest corner. In the second, he assisted Firmino and the match ended up in win for the Reds. Some days after he signed a double while his team had just equalized and defeat Newcastle on a 3-1 score. It was Sadio's fiftieth appearance in Premier League at Anfield, then not to have lost one game since his arrival. This continued till the game against Leicester at home, while the Nanthio opened the score in a 2-1 win. It was his 100th appearance in Premier League under the colors of the Reds and score his fiftieth on November 12th, he saved his team in a crucial game against Aston by scoring the victory goal at the 94th minute and he proved decisive in the following game against, scoring a wonderful goal against Manchester City of Guardiola. Sadio played threesome scoring the first goal for his team in win against the Eagles. On December 4, 2019, he made man of the match's performances through a Merseyside derby winning the match on a 5-1 score. He played crucial roles in the goals of his teammates; Xherdan Shaqiri and

Divock Origi with two perfect deep goal and gave the Reds an advance of 2-0. Just before the end of the first half-time he scored the only and unique goal of the match.

On February 22nd, 2022, Sadio scored the victory goal at the 80th minute of the game, putting Liverpool to twenty-two point ahead Manchester City. The Reds was well on their way Championship title, which they had been pursuing since 1990. Jurgen Klopp's men won the Premier League on June 25 and Mane was selected in the PFA team of the year, after he had scored eighteen goals in championship, that is twenty-two goals in all competitions.

2021-2022, Sadio Mane's Bad Season:

According to Sadio, that season has been the worst of throughout his career so far. Liverpool finished the season without winning the smallest trophy and Sadio scored only 11 goals in Championship. He made a great start of the season by scoring a double during a win against Chelsea before his goals in the following games against Everton and Arsenal. After that, he played 14 games and scored only one goal before breaking the lock against Crystal Palace. Following this score, Mané got better but his general performances were still criticized due to the fact he missed lots of occasions and barely created one. Yet, by the end of the season, he regained shape, scoring four goals in his last seven appearances plus two assists. This included crucial double goal in a 2-0 win, securing his team a participation to the following champions league.

SADIO'S LAST SEASON IN ENGLAND:

On August 21st 2021, opened his goals' account for the new the new season during a win against Burnley. He embarked on an excellent series of goals, scoring nine times during his last thirteen appearances. Yet, he experienced afterward some moments without scoring any goals neither delivering any assist in nine game. He would later break this curse on January 2nd when he scored in a game against Chelsea. That was his last appearance since he had been representing his country in the Africa Cup of Nations.

After his return, and with the signing of Louis Suarez, adding a new option the left row. Mané started to play a central role, operating more and more as a number nine. This brought a slow starting, because in eleven games, Mané just scored four goals since his he had come back. In spite of that, he started and played for eighty minutes during the final game of EFL, the Reds won the game after a sequence of penalty-shoots. On April 5, 2022, Sadio scored the second goal of Liverpool during a 3-1 against Benfica in champions league. Five days, he found the nets equalizing during a draw against Manchester City in the Premier League. He went on with a double against the same team in the finale of the FA cup, this time with a 3-2 win. Three days, the number 10 made one of the best performances with the Reds, scoring a goal contributing to a great 4-0 victory against Manchester United. After that, he scored a goal at each step in the semi-finales of the champions league, when Liverpool defeated Villareal and joined the Champions League Final for the third time since the Senegalese "Nugget" had signed to the club. On May 14, Sadio played for the one hundred and twenty minutes in the final of the FA cup. The match ended up into a 0-0 draw. Then came the time of penalty-shoots and Sadio Mané was among the shooters, but his penalty shot was stopped by the strong Edouard Mendy. Fortunately, the Reds defeated Chelsea after the penalty-shoots and Mané completed his series of major trophies at the Reds' club. Two weeks later, Mané was a starter in the Reds team for the third time in EUFA champions league final. However, this time there was no happy ending for, the Brazilian Vinicus Jr deferred the Reds' dream by scoring the only goal of the match. This appearance turned out to be the last one under the flag of the Reds.

After the final, Sadio Mané showed his intention to leave the club that summer, invoking the necessity of a new challenge. Many big clubs such as Paris Saint Germain, Real Madrid, and Bayern Munich wanted to have Mané in their team. It is therefore without any surprise the biggest German club which would have him on a deal of forty million euro.

    On July 1st, Sadio Mané left Liverpool after having beautifully served the English club. In all, He got 269 appearances, scored 120 goals and made 38 assists. During his stay in the club, he won the Premier League, UEFA champions league, the FA club, FIFA world cup clubs, the EFL cup, and the UEFA super cup, and Sadio has become one of the greatest attackers in the history of the club.

Image 16: Sadio Mane with Liverpool in 2022. His last season with the club

Image 17: Sadio fails for the second time in three years to win the Champions League, a trophy which would be great to him.

Image 18: Bayern Munich, the new club of Sadio Mane. when we started writing this book, Sadio hadn't started his career with Bayern yet. Therefore we don't tackle this deal with the club in this book.

SADIO MANE INSIDE THE DEN OF THE LIONS:

At the end of the campaign with FC Metz, and after twenty appearances with two goals, Sadio received his first Senegal call-up in May 2012. In a game against Morocco on May 25, he honored his first call-up by delivering an assist to Moussa Konate, who score the only goal of the match at the seventy-ninth minute. Then Sadio was substituted by his friend Cheikhou Kouyate, also known in Senegal as "borom Niaari diabar", the man of two espouses. In spite the Teranga Lions' efforts, Morocco win the game on a 2-1 score. Mane scored his first goal with the Senegalese National team, during his second call-up, on June 2nd, 2012 against Liberia and allowed his team to win the match on a 3-1 score. He was very fruitful in the game and his performances were outstanding. His physical strength and his wonderful skills performances won him a place in the Senegal Olympic football team in 2012. Endowed an exemplary vivacity, a nugget of talent, Nanthio is undoubtedly the new hope of the Senegalese. From then all eyes were on him and perhaps he will be the one who will allow Senegal to win their first continental trophy. The is the first time in the history of Senegalese football that an Olympic team has succeeded in participating in an Olympic football. For its entry into the London 2012 Olympic Games, Senegal managed to score a draw against the host country, Great Bretagne. It was not an easy task for Senegal, the Teranga young lions managed to keep their opponent high and sore a draw. Senegal confirmed in the following game by offering Uruguay a score of two goals to zero thanks to a magnificent double by the attacker Moussa Konate. Defender Abdoulaye Diallo was expelled with a red card in the thirty-seventh minute following an unskilled tackle. Despite this numerical inferiority, the young lions were able to resist the attempts of Louis Suarez and Edinson Cavani. Thanks to this great success, Sadio Mané and his teammates overlook their opponents and took the lead of group A. After a draw against the United Arab Emirates still in the group stages, Senegal joined Mexico for the quarter finals.

Trailing 2-0, in the first half time, the young lions come back in the second with much more motivation and get a draw which helps them to go to overtime. Repetitive defensive errors undermined the Senegalese team which ended up taking two other goals. Yet, they had managed to switch the game by equalizing while they were dominated with a 2-0 score at the first half. The child of Bambali, Sadio Mané was in the line-up through all the games and became a key player in the team.

In the world cup playoffs, the Nanthio scored the first goal against Liberia during the first day and the following game he notched a goal for his team in the scope of world cup playoffs. This victory allowed Senegal to play the third round of the playoffs. Senegal was finally eliminated after two matches against Ivory Coast. The Teranga Lions will miss the greatest competition of the planet. The number 10 is viewed as the most important player of the team. The Senegalese people are then convinced to keep Sadio Mané, one of the most talented players of his generation. Dribbles, percussions and technical appropriateness, the new number 10 has all the qualities to become one of the stars of Senegalese football. As rewards of his wonderful performances Sadio Mané was nominated the Senegalese Golden ball. From now the boss of the Senegalese football team. He started then receiving praises. His idol, Elhadj Diouf said that Sadio is the boss of the Senegalese football team in spite of young age, it is he who should pull up the Senegalese national team.

On January 15th, a heavy toll on the Senegalese football team who was deprived of Sadio Mané, after he had been injured on the left tight. His coach Ronald Koeman said that he was going to be forfeited and miss the African cup of nation. But the following day, the national team coach didn't rely on what Koeman had said, eventually Sadio was on the squad of Aliou Cissé, and he ended up going to Equatorial Guinea in order to participate to the African Cup of Nation. Arrived at the 2015 AFCON with an injury, Sadio couldn't help his team avoid an elimination since the second round in Equatorial Guinea. For his first AFCON participation, the Senegalese number 10 left Equatorial Guinea without playing one single minute.

Senegal never crowned champion in African Cup of Nations, but full of ambitions namely brilliant playoffs, no defeat, six victories through six matches. It is through this sense that Senegal gets its ticket to the 2017 AFCON, and the hope is high for the Senegalese fans. Senegal, a country which had been pursuing its first continental trophy would be frustrated at the early group stages. Indeed, Senegal was in the death group which included Algeria and Tunisia. After a hot-headed entrance against Tunisia, Senegal gains a penalty in the second minute that Sadio Mané will transform without any difficulty and some minutes later Kara Mbodj double the lead with a headed goal on a corner then widen the gap. The Senegalese players boosts their confidence after the great win. They just want to forget their early elimination through the group stages in the two last AFCON. to accomplish this, the team rely on the then-Liverpool star in order to go far in the competition.

Senegal did well in the group stages gain two wins and a draw against Algeria of the impressive player Mahrez. Senegal reaches the quarter finals and face Cameroon. A match which sounds like a déja-vu since Senegal had been defeated by Cameroon during the 2002 African cup of Nation. So, for the Senegalese players this match was a remontada of the 2002 AFCON final, that's why they have to do their utmost on the playground in order to win this typical game. The match was a duel of goalies and there was no goal on both sides. The two team went to the penalty-shoots which were at the advantage of Indomitable lions of Cameroon after their goalie had ultimately stopped Sadio Mane's shot. A terrible elimination of Senegal, which however made an impeccable track. The one who might have won the trophy of the best player of the tournament was just heartbroken and inconsolable, and shedding tears of frustration. After he had missed a penalty which eliminated his dear team, it was his whole world which fell apart, the number 10 was devastated, and it took the members of the staff team to help him leave the pitch. It was certainly one of the saddest days for the Nanthio. It is an utter disillusion. Sparkling since the beginning of the competition, Sadio Mané had really led his team to the quarters-final thanks to his fabulous performances. Unfortunate, only his missed penalty against Cameroon will be remembered.

On November 10th Sadio Mane and his band would secure Senegal a second participation to the soccer World cup through a 2-0 win against South Africa. His teammates and him remained undefeated through five matches in these playoffs, they would have the opportunity to join Russia, thus waling on their 2002 elders' steps. An opportunity to forget their disillusionment. On June 19, 2018, Mane and his teammates made their entrance against Poland on a 2-0 score in the presence of Senegalese Republic president Macky SALL, who had come to attend this match. On the second day, Sadio Mané scored his first goal in the world cup against Japan. He was nominated the man of the match after his great performances. The following game was between Senegal and Colombia through the group stages. In order to get their tickets for the quarters-final, the Teranga lions had to win that game. Right from the kick-off Sadio and his teammates heavily attack and position themselves at the top of the playground putting the Colombians under pressure in the half of their pitch. In the sixth minutes Mané takes a march on the Colombia back-marker. Overtaken by Mane, the Colombian tackles Mané who falls down. At a real speed, the referee signals a penalty, bu the VAR (video assistance referee), a tool often unfair to the African team in this world cup, urges the referee to reconsider his decision tough the tackle was contentious. On the wings, Sadio Mane and Ismael Sarr triggered the best opportunities for the lions. It is on bittersweet-taste that Lions left the 2018 World cup after Colombia had notched a goal in the seventh minute and the match ended on a 1-0 score. The saddest in this elimination is that Senegal and Japan had the same points and goal differences. Sadio Mané and his teammates are then eliminated on the numbers of yellow cards accumulated since the beginning of the tournament. And that ends the adventure of the Teranga Lions at the 20218-world cup.

Image 19: 2017 AFCON Quater-finals, Senegal being eliminated by Cameroon at the shootouts, Mane was heartbroken.

Image 20: Stage group match of 2018 world cup, Senegal defeats Poland, the Lions celebrating their win.

Image 21: Senegal vs Japan, second stage group game during the 2018 World Cup. Mane nominated Man of the match, after a 1-1 draw

Image 22: Senegal vs Colombia : 3rd stage group match, the Lions defeated on a 1-0 score. That's the end of the adventure

Still no rewards for this golden generation. In spite of the bitter lived experiences, the Teranga Lions go once again with lot of hope and the sole aim to win this African Cup of Nation. Senegal was in hat 1, thanks to their FIFA classification. After the draw, Senegal shares its group with Algeria, Kenya and Tanzania. This draw is in favor to the Teranga Lions according to the Senegalese Foot Federation. On the first round, Senegal faces Tanzania without the number 10, and the Lions defeat Tanzania without lot of difficulties particularly thanks to Krepin Diatta who wonderfully netted the second goal, and he was also nominated the man of the match. In the second game, Sadio and his teammates were defeated by Algeria on a 1-0 score. The refereeing was perceived as being in favor of Algeria, namely due to a not whistled penalty on Sadio Mané. The Senegalese Team secures their round 16 qualification in the last day of the group stages, largely dominating Kenya thanks to a superb double goal of Sadio Mane who also nominated the man of the match. Without sparkling, Senegalese eliminated Uganda and joined the quarters-final. Again, Sadio led his team forward by netting the only of the match which allows his team to reach the quarters-final to defy Benin. Facing a strong and courageous Benin team but which ends up exploding, and incapable of resisting speed of Sadio Mané and Mbaye Niang who were really hard on the squirrel. The Teranga Lions impose themselves against Benin thanks to a goal of the midfield Idrissa Gana Gueye on an assist of Sadio Mané. It was the only goal of the game which allows Aliou Cissé's men to reach the four of the AFCON since 2006. Being always criticized for not being able play under pressure during great competitions, the 2019 Teranga Lions had so far proved to be astonishingly resilient and strong. At the end of hot-headed and intense game against Tunisia after both teams had missed a penalty, the Teranga Lions had to push to the extra-time in order to get rid of the Carthage Eagles and head straight to the final for the second time in their history. A match waited by the fans of the round ball but above all by the followers of both teams. At the Cairo international stadium, Senegal and Algeria dueled on Friday evening July 19, 2019 for the big final game of the African Cup of nations final. A remake of the group stages match which was worn by the Fennecs of Algeria. On the Senegalese side, Sadio Mané wants to win and bring the cup home for the first time in the history of team who had never won one. Sadio and his teammates hope that this will be the right moment after such moments of disillusionment. In a tense and tight match since the kick-start, the Fennecs netted an early goal, in the seventieth second. Courageous, the Senegalese largely dominated the game, proving to be more insisting and powerful, and never finding the nets. Again, a new disillusionment for Mané and his teammates. The Nanthio was the main danger for the Algerians, compelling them to foul and then stop him. Sadio and his bold gang could not bring the cup but they had won the heart of the Senegalese people. Upon their arrival on the day following their defeat, the lions were triumphantly welcomed by their best supporters who had come to the airport. The Senegalese supporters also followed the Teranga Lions all along their way to the presidential palace where the President and his government members were waiting for them in order to pay them a tribute because they had been great warriors on the pitch and dominated the game. Words fail to describe the ambiance of that day. One could see fans singing and dedicating anthem to the Lions while believing wholeheartedly that Senegal would one day win the African cup of nation. Along the way, the supporters were chanting touchy messages to the attention of the players: *"we don't get daunted, the cup will come one day or another insha'Allah"*. A magnificent support which helped Aliou Cisse and his soldiers to go forward with lot of motivations and sport attitudes.

Finale de la CAN 2019. Sadio Mané en action

Déception de Sadio Mané et des joueurs sénégalais après leur défaite face à l'Algérie en finale de la CAN 2019.

2021-AFCON, THE DAY OF GLORY HAS COME

The litany of failures experienced by Senegal at the African Cup of Nation, had caused teardrops particularly those of the young prodigy, Sadio Mané. But far from being discouraged and wiped out by these failures, the Nanthio did not flinch, on the contrary he became mentally stronger and was never as ready to take up the new challenge. Unsurprisingly, Sadio and his band booked their places in the African Cup of Nations. Considered the favorite team on the paper, the Senegal National team is put at the top by the FIFA classification. It should be noticed that the Senegalese people's expectations were high and justified too. President Macky SALL, who is a football himself said: *"this time, we don't claim a final but we want the cup, the nation has been waiting with great hope for so many years"*. A prize list which was so far empty for the Senegalese national team. The lions don't get discouraged and remain convinced that impossible is not Senegalese. They intend to continue their hunt despite the accumulated failures. Senegal is in group B with Zimbabwe, Malawi, and Guinea Conakry. Troubled and disturbed by the Covid-19 pandemic, Aliou was deprived of many of his starting line-up players during their opening matches in the 2022 AFCON. Classified as the favorite team of the competition, Aliou Cisse's players didn't frighten and were able to defeat Zimbabwe only in the last minutes thanks to a goal of Sadio Mane. The men of Aliou Cisse cruelly lack realism and dynamism in the faces of goals. Though all great players had joined the team then, Sadio Mané and his teammates don't find the nets through the two following games, but still they validate their ticket for the eighth-finals. Senegal then knew by which way they had to pass in the pursuit of their first continental trophy. After they finished first in their group, The Teranga Lions had to play against Cape Vert in the eighth-finals. Determined to show another image of themselves after a tough and delicate group stage. Sadio and his teammates attacked in the early minutes of the match. As an exemplary playmaker, the number 10 of Senegal's Lions, Sadio Mané showed the way by hitting the pole after a beautiful collective movement. After this nice occasion, the corners multiply for the Teranga Lions, but efficiency was still lacking. Already favorite in this game, Senegal gets a numerical superiority after the exclusion of Cape Vert midfield due to a heavy sole on Senegalese midfield Pape Gueye. In fifty-seventh minute, on a hazardous output of the Cape Vert goalie who hit Sadio Mané, after checking the Video Referee Assistance, the central referee decides, a new red card for the Cape Vert goalie. Though he was in bad shape, Sadio Mané resisted till the end. Outnumbered nine to eleven, the Crioulos of Cape Vert become much less intense in their gameplay. After a corner poorly cleared, Sadio retrieves the ball and opened the score thanks to a shot bouncing under the bar. Still shaken after his shock with the Cape Vert goalie, Sadio Mané ended up leaving the pitch due to the hurt he felt on his head. In a completely unblanched game, the Senegalese showed patience and realism and sealed the win thanks to the efficiency of the young prodigy Bamba Dieng who doubled the score in the ninety-second minute. After that victory, Senegal had as adversary Equatorial Guinea with the hope of having reassuring news from their star Sadio Mané who didn't finish the previous match because of an injury. The Lions' playmaker is uncertain. Neither him nor the staff know if he is able to play the next game. Whatever the case the *Nanthio* is ready to risk his life to honor his dear country. He tells this difficult moment: *"when I was injured, this cerebral contusion, it was a hard time.*

There were Covid-19 cases, the pitch conditions, the altitude for me, the problem for me was to change the hours of the match for me. But when I got the injury on the head, I was scared. But the worst in that Liverpool put the pressure. They wrote to the FIFA a letter saying that the injury requires five days of rest. That means I had not to play the quarters-final. There was our team physician who also should respect the rules. I was in my room, they told me that I had not to play the quarters-final, I immediately called the coach and told him that it was ou of question, he had to put in the line-up because I was going to play. He said Ok, he would talk to the physician. I immediately called the Senegalese Foot Federation President to tell that we had to organize a meeting. For me, it was important to play that match, I could even give my life. We met four an hour and I told them to make a contract for me to sign in case I die, that will be my fault. Finally, I didn't sign the paper. They did a CAT can on the day of the match and sent it to the AFC (African Confederation of Football) to let them know that I was ready to play". These words convey Sadio's a sense of self-sacrifice, and love of his country. A real patriot, he ready for whatever to honor and defend the flag of his dear Senegal. With Sadio in the line-up, Senegal began tentatively the game. At the top of the pitch, the Guinean player started troubling the Senegalese. But the Teranga Lions finally find the nets just before half an hour on a wonderful assist of Sadio Mané to Famara Diediou. This later on the Guinean defense, opened his left foot and put the ball on the left corner of the nets. In a crazy atmosphere, the match ended on a 3-1 score in favor of Senegal. At the end of the match, the number 10 of the Senegalese team, who is accustomed to duels with his club, Liverpool, said: *"now the objective is to go all the way in order to win this trophy that we dearly take to heart."*

The outcome is close, facing Burkina Faso in the semi-finales at Amadou Ahidjo stadium of Yaoundé, Senegal kicked off this crucial match. The beginning of the match turned out rather stuttering and faulty. The twenty actors get separated at the half time on a draw. At the return from the changing rooms, no substitution had been made. Since the early minutes of the game, Senegal began to strongly attack the Burkinabe who were retreating in their thirty meters. Some minutes later, Aliou made a replacement with the arrival of Ismail Sarr and Pape Gueye who respectively substituted Famara

Diediou and Cheikhou Kouyaté. These substitutes came at the right time and befitted the Lions who would quickly open the nets. Autor of good breakthrough, Ismail Sarr gets a corner. Bouna Sarr shots the corner and finds Koulibaly, who tries an overhead kick. On the trajectory, Abdou Diallo controls the ball with his thigh, turns over with a powerful strike. The Lions open the score. In the following Minutes, Burkina Faso suffers terribly and increasingly back down. The stallions of the country of honest men end up cracking. After the adversary team's loss of ball, Sadio Mane retrieves the round leather, he overflows along the goal line in the penalty-area before centering the ball for Idrissa Gana Gueye who springs up at the first pole in order to cut the trajectory of the ball and mislead the Burkinabe goalie, worsening the score to 2-0. The break is made. Yet, the Stallions didn't give up, they were completely in the game then. Authors of beautiful ball pick-ups, the Burkinabe players go on a counter-attack. On the right-side Bertrand Traore sends the ball to his teammate Issa Kaboré who then gives the ball to Blati Touré who springs up and sends the ball to deep inside the nets of the Senegalese goalie. But that is not enough, because Senegal widen the gap some minutes later through a counter-attack finished by Sadio Mané who mislead the Faso goalie and shoots the ball with a perfect left lob. We could see 3-1 in favor of Senegal on the big display panel of the stadium. At the end of pleasant and unbridled game, the Senegal of Sadio Mané brings Burkina Faso to the knees in the last four of the African cups of nations. For their second consecutive time, after the one lost in 2019, the Teranga Lions, then more seasoned and convinced had to face the great Egypt of Mohamed. In any fashion, only victory counts. The Teranga Lions are in a mission in the Cameroon land: snatch that devilish star from an African cup of nations which had been cruelly escaping since their very participation to this tournament in 1965. To make it happen, Senegal, the big favorite of this duel game, can rely on their ever-smiling guide: Sadio Mané, a crazy class player, with a confusing fair-play. A delicacy in each shot, a sensitivity which can felt even to stands. His kindness should not make the exceptional forward forget that he is on the pitch with his dizzying flashes, his fiery dribbles and overthrowing shots. Sadio Mané alone, can shift the turn of bad game. Joseph Lopy emphasizes this on Sadio Mane: *"he gives us the taste of the high level, because when we see him working, we realize that maybe we are not working enough and we must be on it".*

Sadio Mané at 29 years old is the incarnation the ultimate dream of any Senegalese football player: to become professional. To add to the dramaturge, the final opposes two teammates of the Premier League, namely in the Liverpool team: The Senegalese Sadio Mané and the Egyptian Mohamed Salah. They are real teammates but also rivals on the international level. Senegal starts well the game. In the third minute, Gueye as playmaker, alerts Saliou Ciss on the left wing. The left-back speeds up and gets inside the penalty-area before falling down after a tackle from an Egyptian defense. Without hesitation, the referee signals a penalty. Knowing his teammates from Liverpool, Mohamed Salah gives some pieces of advises to their goalie in order to stop the shot of Mané who obviously takes up his responsibilities. Mané takes a swing and sends strong the ball on the right side of Gabaski, the Egyptian goalie. Gabaski went on the good side, made a phenomenal parade to keep his nets inviolate.

Senegal dominates the match with more ball possessions while Egypt play on the defense as they know it by keep the game close in order to slow down their adversary rhythm. The Teranga Lions manage however to create some occasions. Back from the restrooms, it is Senegal that still carries the ball forward and multiplies dangerous situations. In spite of some chills in the second half, neither Senegal nor Egypt manage to break the adversary lock. And despite the overtime minutes, the score remains unchanged. The two team will therefore decide in the overtimes. After thirty of overtimes, the score was still blank. A real goalies' duel, which will end up in penalty-shots. After Egypt missed two penalties, Sadio Mané showed up again in front of Gabaski' "wall" and shot his penalty with all the energy and power he had. The Egyptian goalie threw himself on the right side but this time he could nothing against the shot of Ali neither change the fate of the Pharaohs. At the end of the night and a suspense the Teranga Lions of Senegal impose themselves on the Egyptians after the penalty-shots session and clinch the African Cup of Nations for the first time in their history. Some minutes later, we could see Sadio Mané solacing his friend and teammate Mohamed Salah who was shedding tears. An attitude which confirms that Sadio is a high-class player. This time, Sadio Mane and his crew have conquered the demons of the round ball. The course of history has been rectified with this triumph. Senegal has finally got its first continental trophy. Sadio has been a driving force behind that victory, and it is one of the best moments of his career as he affirms at the end of the match and after have lifted the most prestigious cup, which indeed had passed on the hands of Africa's great legends such as Abedi Pelé, Roger Mila, Rabah Madjer, Jay-Jay Okocha to new but a few, " *this emotion is grandiose. It is the first time that it has happened to me with such*

Image 25: One can see on these images the decisive penalty of Sadio Mane, and Mané embracing the cup which he had been so much dreaming about, then the joy of Senegalese players and finally the atmosphere in Dakar after final whistle and Monday 6 declared a public and paid holiday in Senegal

an intensity. It was so strong that it took me some time to realize that it was true. As if things puzzling inside my head. By seeing the ball shaking the nets, I have had feelings that I have never had before. With an unbelievable force. And then, as I was over the moon, I remember Idrissa Gana coming to me hugging and squeezing me saying "we made it", "we did it Sadio. I was like dreaming. I didn't want to wake up. I have already won a UEFA championship League, 2019 clubs World Cup, and the Premier League in 2020. Bu this one! It is the best so far! I can't an hour without thinking about it to such a point that when I call my friends, I can't help telling them, "hey my bro, we have won the AFCON". Tears, cries, crazy laughers sweep across the capital city of Dakar and all around the country. As everywhere in Senegal, thousands of people, men and women, young men and aged-men, all of them have attended to the historical coronation of the Teranga Lions in the final game of the AFCON against Egypt on February 6.

In this indescribable joy atmosphere for many supporters one can see the admiration all these people have for their national team led charismatic coach Aliou Cisse. A new generation of international football players. Music, chants, and horns sounded until late at night to show the fervor of the AFCON over the course of the game and the hope it had triggered in Senegal. To allow all the Senegalese to take fully advantage of the event and show the proud of the whole nation, the following day, namely Monday 7 February, was declared a public holiday in Senegal by the President of Republic.

SADIO MANE, THE PHILANTROPE

Apart from his excellent sportive performances, Sadio has a huge impact in the development of his home village of his region and even his country. In spite of his outstanding prize list, Sadio Mané is humble and humanist athlete. He is never reluctant in terms of philanthropy and charitable works so little as they are. His fortune is far from turning the head of the young man who managed to keep his head on his shoulders and his feet on the ground. The native of Bambali uses his time and money to solace people's sufferings. Sadio is not like those excessive squanderers who show up with luxuries. This young Senegalese's way of life and daily activities have almost surprised everybody because despite of billions of dollars he has always stayed true to himself and his limited-resources origins. He always provides his people with the necessary means. The Senegalese star doesn't hesitate to make donations to make his loved ones happy. Contrary to many football players of his calibers, who invest their fortune in buying branded clothes and luxury automobiles. Sadio thinks that a smile can change the fate of someone for good. Then he does all that he can to put a smile on the faces of his loved ones. Outside of the playground, the Senegalese number has always proved his capacity as an excellent manager of humans and resources, as well as a youth mobilizer. He is concerned about the wellbeing pf his community by carrying out humanitarian projects in different parts of Senegal. His donations and helps go not only to his family and close ones but also to all his home village. Sadio doesn't count when it comes to helping to most needy, a precious and authentic support because it comes from someone who has gone through the same misery and the daily hardships. His charitable works provides sufficient evidence how the application of the devotion to the fight against poverty through donations and projects can bring a support which changes lives. An up-standing citizen and hero for Senegal, the charitable works of Sadio Mané continue to show their iconicity throughout Senegal.

A WELL EQUIPED HOSPITAL FOR HIS HOME VILLAGE

The father of Sadio Mané passed away when Sadio was young, since then the lack of sanitary services in his home village has become an important cause in the life of the football player. He also remembers the difficult birth of his sister at their home because at that time they didn't sanitary services in their locality. They two events remain etched in the memory the Senegal' star. So, in order to avoid that such tragedies to happen again and to help others not experience these difficult such misfortune, Sadio Mané has paid out an amount of five hundred thousand dollars for the building of a new hospital in his home village. The superstar has even met the president of the Senegal Republic Macky SALL in order to submit his ambitious project, suggesting the latter to provide the hospital with a medical staff. The official president account tweeted: *"the forward of Liverpool has present to the president of the Republic an ambitious building plan and bank on the support of the state for a medical stuff"*. Sadio mane then attended to the opening of the hospital, settled in Bambali. Well build and equipped, this hospital can receive and host all the patients from Bambali and from the 34 surrounding villages. Following Nanthio's hard personal experiences with poverty during his childhood and the painful birth of his sister, the hospital will hold a maternity section. These expressions of women from his native village show the pride and the gratitude that the inhabitants of Bambali have for their blessed child: *"He spent all his all his childhood here in Bambali till the day when the fate has driven elsewhere. We thank him days and nights and we pray that God grant him His blessings. I have just come from the nursery; it is thanks to him that we are treated at home without many difficulties and at the lowest costs. I am really happy"*.

If he is generous, Sadio Mane is equally very discrete on the question, in a time of modesty on his part. We can also say that the millions of dollars he wins hasn't really gone to his head. He has indeed a modesty lifestyle. He prefers to help and support his loved ones who are really in need. So humbly that the native of Bambali refrains from doing futile and nonsense things with his own money and prefers to use it for a cause. His maternal aunt said something on this matter: *"thanks God, I am the sister of Sadio's mother and we really thank him for all the things he has done and we equally pray that the Almighty preserves him from the evil forces, this house you see over there has been built by Sadio Mané, he is certainly the son of Satou and Karamoko but Mané is everybody's Mané. May God protect and him more and more."*

Image 26: Bambal's hospital financed by Sadio Mane about 500, 000 euros (or around 33 million CFA)

Image 27: Sadio Mane during the inauguration of the hospital in Bambali

A HUGE AMOUNT OF MONEY FOR BUILDING A HIGH SCHOOL IN BAMBALI

"Education is the most powerful weapon to change the world", Nelson would say. Sadio has really understood that statement in spite of young age. Knowing the importance of education, Sadio Mané has built many classrooms and a wall to fence off the school. Charitable works that let nobody indifferent in his native village. One can see the pride and respect on the faces of Bambali inhabitants when it comes to talking about the number 10 of Senegal's National football team and above all of his achievements. One of the teachers at Bambali high school for which Sadio Mané has built classrooms attests to Sadio Mane's generosity and devotion of the Bambali native: *"We started high school with two state-built buildings, after we united the high school and the junior school, and we were obliged to stay in the*

same spot, that is the reason why we had a problem of classrooms and when the principal of the high came, he tried to start working on the buildings issue with the available mean, it is only afterwards that our star Sadio Mané who took it from here, he distributed an amount of about one hundred and fifty millions in order to build us ten classrooms, and with that money we have able to finish building three classrooms that we had started. He has also built a library and administrative constructions". On top of that, he made a donation of computers to the students of his village in order to help them stay focused on their studies.

After the 2019-African Cup of Nations, while all the football players left for their different countries, Sadio Mané rather than spending his time flattering, showing off his wealth and going to the most luxurious towns of the world to enjoy his holidays as many football players of his age do, he moved from one project to another on his arrival to Senegal to check the extent of the work done in the hospital, the mosque and the school that he was building for the inhabitant of his community. In addition to his humanitarian services, he also distinguished himself by offering football kits to the children of his home village. He also provided financial support to some needy family which cannot meet their needs. Sadio has really understood that being kind and staying close to where we come from does not cost anything. People cannot help falling in love with Sadio's good actions which are in favor of a contribution and positive development in the community from which he comes. The football star does not hesitate to do the maximum of money donations but also of himself, for instance, when he was seen on a picture cleaning the toilettes of Liverpool mosque where he would go and pray. It is not easy to be as modest and fervent as Mané.

Sadio Mane's philosophy is not only about winning football games but also helping others who are in need of financial and other kind of supports. During the 2021 African cup of nations in Cameroon, Senegal was playing against Cape Vert when Sadio had a concussion after a shock with the goalie of Cape Vert which eventually drove him to a hospital in the region of Bafoussam. He met a family who child was seriously injured after being hit by a motorbike. Unable to pay the medical fees, Sadio went closer to them in order to ask what was going on, and after a short discussion he gave them an amount of four hundred thousand CFA for the child's medical fees.

Image 28: Bambali high school

Image 29: Sadio Mane receiving thanks from Bambali students for this magnificent high school which will allow them to further their secondary studies in their region and not to live in difficult conditions in the cities of the country

SENEGALESE YOUNG WOMEN'S EMPOWERMENT

Sadio Mane's charitable works have made him the ambassador of *THE TO PLAY,* an international nonprofit organization whose mission is to empower vulnerable and at-risk children. He collaborated with the organization in order to secure the empowerment the equality and empowerment of women in Senegal, by sensitizing them on the importance for them to be able to access to sportive and educative opportunities on the same footing with men. This work is profitable in Senegal, a country where women are daily facing a lack of opportunities in the fields of finance and education. The above-mentioned organization has implemented a capacity building program for girls through sport. It employs the power of sport to promote gender equality and the rights of teenagers and young women in the country with the philanthropic work of Sadio Mané.

In his efforts to revive his community, Sadio Mané has funded the opening of a gas station, a post office, along with offering scholarships and computers to the students from Bambali. He has also given sport equipment, the access to Internet and even a monthly allowance to families in Bambali. Sadio Mane has always stayed close to his relatives and loved ones, and the media ask him questions about this matter, he politely turns them down. He doesn't give out his money in order to be famous. He only wants to share with his community the chance and opportunity he has got to in life to have as much money to practice the sport that he is really passionate about. It is not easy to find a player as inspiring as Sadio Mané.

Image 30: Sadio Mane in his role as an ambassador for Right to Play

RESTORING THE MOSQUE OF BAMBALI:

Great football player, a respectful and serious man, Sadio Mané is also a fervent Muslim, who is very devoted to his religious and social education. Therefore, his charitable works also go in to the religious field. Indeed, one year before the building of the high school, Sadio Mane had undertaken, still in his home village, the restoring of a mosque estimated at fifty million CFA. An action which has been saluted by the Muslim community. The imam of the village sincerely thanked him and prayed God to safeguard him. There is no doubt that his late father will be proud of him. Contrary to many players who hide their Muslim identity, Sadio Mané is indeed proud of it because he knows that each of our identities which are part and parcel of our personality brings more to our humanism and we should be aware of it and use this identity for promoting peace, peaceful coexistence and love between all the human beings on earth. That is the reason he is often seen bowing down and thanking God whenever he scores a goal especially in the big European stadiums where people usually don't have a good image of the Muslim because of the negative propaganda which Islam often subjected to.

A STADIUM IN SADIO MANE'S NAME

Together with football stars such as his idol Elhadj Diouf, Papis Demba Cissé, Mbaye and Diagne, Sadio Mané delights his fans from Bambali by playing a football game them in the rain on a symbolic spot for the best scorer of Senegal national team. As a matter of fact, it is the place where he had started playing football during his childhood. This is what Sadio said about this fabulous moment: *"I have played again on the playground with more pleasure. I have really enjoyed playing in the rain on the playground of Bambali. My former teammates did the request"*. Besides, it is at the end of the match that the double African Golden Ball Winner decided to build a new infrastructure for his locality.

Image 31: The New stadium of Sedhiou in Casamance which is being built and is going to be name after Sadio Mane. All gratitude for the child of Bambali

INDIVIDUAL DISTINCTIONS:

From Senegal to England, via France and Austria, Sadio Mané has won an impressive number of trophies both collectively and individually. If he has made good days with the European teams, Sadio Mané has definitely imposed himself as the Senegal best player of the decade by winning the Senegalese golden ball from 2014 to 2019. The Nanthio has kept the bar high since he has appeared to the general public.

For his first campaign at Liverpool in England, Sadio Mané was nominated "Talent of Gold" by the Canal + broadcast "Africa's Talents". He has won the prize after a great season of 27 games with 13 goals and 6 assists with Liverpool. Whenever he scored one or two goals during a, his team came out victorious of the game. The 2019 has been indeed the most explosive so far in his career. That very yearn Sadio distinguished himself as being one the most impressive forwards among the explosive trio with Mohamed Salah and Firmino. Sadio had a splendid season in 2019 at Liverpool. And only the statistics can prove that Sadio Mane's year was extraordinary. In the Premier League, he has played 36 games, delivered six assists and won 30 games. He has been a pillar for his team in their pursuit of the champions League and allowed them to lift the trophy after having scored five goals and delivered two assists. Without forgetting his super star role in the Senegalese national team. Sadio and his teammates had reached the AFCON final, but they were unlucky against Algeria in the final. The Nanthio's evolution is impressive during these last years, and even whispered that he would be the 2019 France Football golden ball as a way of awarding his great season, but he ended at the fourth position after, the great Ronaldo, his teammates Virgil, and the winner Lionel Messi. 22nd, then 23rd position during his first two nominations, Mane the positioned 4$^{th.}$ Not far off the podium, which was frustrating for him indeed. Light but not too much, Sadio is that hero who runs into darkness after having saved his world. A year during which he won the champions league, the super cup, world cup clubs, ended up vice champion of England, AFCON vice champion, and joint-top in the premier league. A resume that is not apparently convincing to win the golden ball. A ranking which has made lot of ink flow

. Many people raised their voices to denounce this scandal of the ranking of the Senegalese who had made an exceptional year and could have been on the podium. A disappointment for the one who hoped that his AFCON journey in Egypt would open him the doors of the trophy. Since George Weah, the Liberian forward won it in 1995, no African player has won it so far. Probably and without any surprise, he won the African golden ball in 2019 and became therefore, the second Senegalese player to receive this trophy behind his role model Elhadji Diouf.

Most recently, Sadio Mané ranked second after Karim Benzema for the 66th Golden Ball edition. It is first time for an African player since the coronation of George Weah, winner of the prestigious sesame in 1995.

SECOND TIME AFRICAN GOLDEN BALL:

The Senegalese football foot team number 10 has accomplished great things throughout the year both with his Senegal's national football team and the most important championships. Sadio Mané has been pivotal in championship and specially during the most difficult moments in the pursuit of the title or in champions league as the most persistent offensive element of the Reds during the season. But it is really thanks to the AFCON won by Senegal that he was awarded the prize. Scoring the win penalty, Sadio Mané did not fail to lead his country to throughout the competition. As evidenced by his three goals and his two assists, but also his state of mind when he breaks the deadlock against Cape Vert during the eighth's finals while he was suffering from a cerebral trauma after a violent shock. Even though Senegal is known as a leading country of the continent, it has never lifted this trophy. Inside such an epic, Mané, the forward leader, has really played his role of leader. For many observers this title is associated with him. He also qualified his country to the 2022world cup by transforming the crucial penalty during the play-offs against the Egypt of Mohamed Salah. This year is definitely that of Sadio Mane, an excellent year rich in success and in thrills. After an XXL season, Sadio Mané has also won the trophy of the best African player of the year at the 2022 CAF Awards. Undoubtedly, the Senegalese has outperformed his teammate Mohamed Salah and his fellowman Edouard Mendy. For Sadio, the sky is the limit, he wants to win more in the coming year. The 30-year-old Senegalese forward strongly believe to be able to go get the record held by the international Ivorian Yaya Touré and Samuel Eto'o, who have respectively four titles. *"First of all, I would like to thank all my teammates, the staff, my club, and especially the national team. I also thank everyone for their support. How to forget our Senegalese fans. They have been great from the beginning to support us to win the AFCON but also to qualify for the 2022 world cup. To the Senegalese journalists who are here with us, I thank you, we have gone everywhere together. When I was younger, the fact of watching the CAF Awards pushed me to work harder to win this trophy. I have come from a long way. I am not articulate and vocal but I am still hungry and I am going to try harder until the last day of career. Records are made to be broken, so why not try again. Sometimes, you can say it's impossible, but for me, it's possible. I will employ all the means necessary to go as far as possible in this coming world cup, but above all try to win another AFCON with Senegal. Yes, we can. Together, with my teammates, we will fight and work hard to make the Senegalese people prouder. We are not going to stop here, that's the very beginning. Today, win must be in DNA of Senegal, it must be the blood that runs in our veins. Therefore, I will do and give the maximum for my country",* Sadio Mané said.

2022 GOLDEN BALL, MANE ALWAYS HIGHER

This season full of achievements, fostered him candidate to the Golden Ball, and Sadio Mané was in ballot with Karim Benzema at the dawn of the big-eared cup final. Yet, once lost, the is new title of the Merengue club make the French international unanimous as his season was impressive between his results both in terms of individual performances and collective ones, namely at the direct elimination of the champions league. Sadio ranked second at the Golden Ball classification after Karim Benzema winner of the 2022 edition. He becomes then the first African football player to reach the podium of this prestigious distinction after George who won it in 1995. The African continent has known football players with such an international dimension but never has a player from the continent been excellently classified since the time of George Weah. 27 years later and on top of names such as Didier Drogba, Samuel Eto'o or Yaya Touré, Mané has updated history by becoming since the creation of the Golden Ball, the second African football player to be on the podium, after ranking 4th in 2019. Senegal and Africa have every reason to be proud of Sadio Mané for all he has accomplished in terms of sport. Sadio, with his talent keep on promoting his country. He highly contributes to the success of his clubs, by bringing there a dynamism infused with hard work, ethic and self-denial. He preaches an example that ends up being an inspiration model for his teammates. There is a reason why the Reds' captain perceives Mané 's departure as the missing link of Liverpool machine. The Senegalese playmaker look farther ahead and believe from now on to win the most prestigious individual awards for a football player.

FIRST WINNER OF SOCRATES PRIZE

The Bambali child has done extraordinary things in terms of football, breaking lots of records, but his best works are humanitarian and social. Thanks to the possibilities he has got as a talented football player, Mané has managed to mobilize around him in order to carry out initiatives that of a great community importance and of a priceless value. His investments in the fields of education and health, and betterment of the populations' living conditions are to commend. They constitute a great lesson for anyone in a position of power or influence that it is only investments in people and the improvement of their dignity that are worth. During the 2022 France Football's Golden Ball ceremony, Sadio has received the Socrates Prize for the first time in the history of football. This trophy awards football players who are engaged in societal and charitable projects. *"Thank you everybody. I am so glad to be here, and if sometimes I can be so shy, I am really happy to do all that for the people at home, in Senegal, for making their lives better. I am delighted of winning this title. As I said, it is an especial prize for me. This motivates me to give the best of me outside of the playground. It was a child dream to do the maximum for those who are around me. I know where I come from, I know the reality. I try to do what I can, the best possible."* Said Sadio Mané during the ceremony.

Apart from his individual distinctions, Sadio Mané holds other records that will be listed in the next pages. 111 goals without any penalty. Such is the succeeded performance of these seasons with Southampton then Liverpool by Sadio Mané. Any other football player evolving in the great five championships hasn't scored such goals without shooting a penalty on the same period. This fact made the best scorer in the history of the English championship without even shooting a single penalty. The Nanthio is the only football player who has scored nine consecutive times against the same opponent in the Premier League history. He has made the same performance with Senegal's national team. In fact, on June 4, 2022 at Abdoulaye Wade stadium, against Benin during the first day of the 2023 AFCON qualifications, Sadio became the best scorer of Senegal's national football team with 32 goals, after his triplet. He then outnumbered Henry Camara who had held the record of the best scorer of Senegal's football team. He also the best decisive figure of the national team too, as the one who has made the most assist so far in the history of Senegal team. With fifteen goals in the final stages of the Champions League, Mane keeps on making the history of the African continent and that of champions league by becoming the best African scorer in the champions league's final stage unseating the Ivorian Didier Drogba. To name but a few of his records, the Nanthio is far from accomplishing his mission and intend to fill with prize list since he is still young.

To finish this book, we wish Sadio Mane all every success that a football player can get on the pitches and podiums. All the best Nanthio! Go far lion!

Image 32:. Sadio Mane, 2022, African golden ball. Another prize

Image 33: Sadio has received the Socrates prize from Rai, brother of the Brazilian legend who passed away in 2011 at the gate of 57. Mane has received this prize thanks to his humanitarian works in Senegal (P. La Halle/L'équipe..

SOURCES

www.wiwsport.com

www.jeuneafrique.com

www.wikipedia.com

www.borgenmagazine.com

www.bigissue.com

www.kpjevents.com

www.liverpoolfc.fandom.com

www.fourfourtwo.com

www.planetfootball.com

www.africafootunited.com

www.sofoot.com

www.sportmagazine.levif.be

www.sudquotidien.sn

www.doingbuzz.com

frceleb-true.com

footmercato.com

lifebooger.net

https://www.lequipe.fr/Football/Article/Sadio-mane-premier-prix-socrates-de-l-histoire-coeur-du-senegal/1359942

TABLE OF CONTENT

2002 WORLD CUP, THE SOURCE OF INSPIRATION 5

CHILDHOOD AND YOUTH OF SADIO MANE 8

THE RUNNING AWAY 9

TOWARDS THE PROFESSIONAL WORLD 10

MANE IN THE WORLD OF PROFESSIONAL FOOTBALL PLAYERS. His beginnings with FC Metz in France 12

A POLISHED DIAMOND AT SALZBURG IN AUSTRIA 15

A SHOOTING STAR IN ENGLAND 18

SADIO MANE IN THE PREMIER LEAGUE HISTORY: 19

MANE AT LIVERPOOL 21

2018-2019, SADIO MANE'S GLORIOUS SEASON: 24

2021-2022, Sadio Mane's Bad Season: 27

SADIO'S LAST SEASON IN ENGLAND: 27

SADIO MANE INSIDE THE DEN OF THE LIONS: 29

2021-AFCON, THE DAY OF GLORY HAS COME 35

SADIO MANE, THE PHILANTROPE 41

A WELL EQUIPED HOSPITAL FOR HIS HOME VILLAGE 42

A HUGE AMOUNT OF MONEY FOR BUILDING A HIGH SCHOOL IN BAMBALI 43

SENEGALESE YOUNG WOMEN'S EMPOWERMENT 45

RESTORING THE MOSQUE OF BAMBALI: 46

A STADIUM IN SADIO MANE'S NAME 47

INDIVIDUAL DISTINCTIONS: 47

SECOND TIME AFRICAN GOLDEN BALL: 49

2022 GOLDEN BALL, MANE ALWAYS HIGHER 50

FIRST WINNER OF SOCRATES PRIZE 51

Summary:

Born in Bambali, a village located in the region of Sedhiou, in the South of Senegal, Sadio is still young when he discovers the enchanting charms of the round ball. Since his early childhood, he only swore by the football, he really fell on love with love it. Sadio Mané knew very well that his chances of becoming a professional football were very limited in his home town. The Nanthio as he is nicknamed, decided to run away and left for Dakar, the Senegalese capital city, in order to a get a place in the football training centers. Seeing that their beloved Sadio was ready for anything including the fact of risking his own life by travelling alone and without any resources, the family of Sadio ended up approving the way that their child wanted to follow. This is how started the adventure of the golden boy who is going to make his way an become one of the greatest forwards in the world. From Generation Foot (a football training center in Senegal), via Bundesliga in Germany, passing by the French League 1, then Austria and later the English Premier League Sadio has won an impressive number of trophies both individually and collectively. An unmatched and exceptional leader, Sadio has managed with his teammates to put a smile on the face of the Senegalese people by giving their first continental trophy with the 2022 AFCON which Senegal had been waiting for years. Unrivalled citizen, and national hero, Sadio Mané is a great humanitarian who is really involved in the in development of his country by implementing important projects and charitable works. As a young professional football player, Sadio Mané has already impressed the world and won many prizes with his country, his club and individually.

The Author:

Ousmane Ba is a young Senegalese student at the department of Economics at Cheikh Anta Diop University of Dakar. As a great football fan and follower, Ousmane wants not only to share and spread the unmatched trajectory of Sadio Mané, but also immortalize this great man both with his performances on the pitch and his humanitarian achievements. An exemplary role model for our young people. He is a living legend and inspiration for the African youth, either in the world of football or not.

www.ingramcontent.com/pod-product-compliance
Lightning Source LLC
Chambersburg PA
CBHW041526090426
42736CB00035B/20